border-crosser with a lamborghini dream

camino del sol

a chicana and chicano

literary series

The University of Arizona Press

Tucson

border-crosser

crosser

poems by Juan Felipe Herrera

with a

lamborghini

dream

The University of Arizona Press
© 1999 Juan Felipe Herrera
First Printing

∞ This book is printed on acid-free, archival-quality paper.
Manufactured in the United States of America.

04 03 02 01 00 99   6 5 4 3 2 1

Library of Congress Cataloging-in-Publication Data
Herrera, Juan Felipe.
Border-crosser with a Lamborghini dream: poems/Juan Felipe Herrera.
p.   cm.   – (Camino del sol)
ISBN 0-8165-1931-5 (acid-free paper)
ISBN 0-8165-1932-3 (pbk.: acid-free paper)
1. Mexican Americans–Poetry. I. Title. II. Series.
PS3558.E74 B67   1999
811'.54–ddc21   98-25480
CIP

British Library Cataloguing-in-Publication Data
A catalogue record for this book is available from the British Library.

Publication of this book is made possible in part by the proceeds of a
permanent endowment created with the assistance of a Challenge Grant
from the National Endowment for the Humanities, a federal agency.

For my children:

Almasol
Joaquín
Joshua
Marlene
& Roberto—
new speakers.

Para siempre, Maga

contents

punk half panther

punk half panther

for Oloberto & Magritta, my Geminis, for Ginsberg

Lissen
to the whistle of night bats—
oye como va,
in the engines, in the Chevys
& armed Impalas, the Toyota gangsta'
monsters, surf of new world colony definitions
& quasars & culture prostars going blam

                over the Mpire, the once-Mpire, carcass
neural desires for the Nothing. i amble
outside the Goddess mountain. Cut across
the San Joaquin Valley, Santiago de Cuba,
Thailand & Yevtusenko's stations;
hunched humans snap off cotton heads
gone awry & twist
nuclear vine legs.

Jut out to sea, once again—this slip
sidewalk of impossible migrations. Poesy mad
& Chicano style undone wild.

Rumble boy. Rumble girl.
In wonder & amazement. On the loose.
Cruisin' shark-colored maze of presidential bombast, death
enshrined archipelago fashion malls, neutered wars
across the globe come barreling down
on my Neo-American uzzi mutations, my upgraded
2Pac thresholds. My indigo streets, i say

with disgust & erotic spit, Amerikkaner frontier consciousness
gone up long ago. Meet my barriohood, meet me
with the froth i pick up everyday & everyday
i wipe away with ablution & apologia & a smirk, then
a smile on my Cholo-Millennium liberation jacket.

No motha', no fatha',
no sista', no brotha'.
Just us in the genetic ticktock
culture chain, this adinfinitum, clueless Americana
grid of inverted serapes, hallucinations of a nation,
streets in racist Terminator
coagulation.

Get loose
after the dayglow artery of a fix.
Power outages propel us into cosmos definition,
another forty-million-New-Dollar-Plantation Basilica,
or is it tender chaos?

My upside-down
Kahlúa gallon *oración* drool
blackish metal flake desires, the ooze of Dulcinea—
Tepeyac Stripper, honey
from Tara's open green fans. Tara?

Tara, where are you?
Tara of the blessings & weapons against illusion.
Against administrator pig,
against molester snake,
against rooster corporate lust. Remember me?
i am the black-red blood spark worker,
Juana Buffalo's illegitimate flight usher,
back up from *Inframundo*.

Quick ooze again,
this formless city space
i live in—
my circular false malaria.

Fungi Town says everything's awright
without your Holy Wheel,

your flaming tree wombs, this sista' bundle
i ache for, the one i lost

in a fast brawl for redemption
at the gates of this Creation Mulatto Hotel,
this body passage, this wonder
        fire from the chest.

i stand alone on Mass Man Boulevard.
Look east, look south. Bleary sirens
come howling with vats of genocide &
gray prison gang buses jam
with my true brotha' wetbacks.

Pick another bale of tropical grape,
another bushel of pesticide & plutonium artichoke.
Cancer tomatoes the biggest in the world.
Bastard word, *bracero* produce, Alien culture—

                                        power & slime.
Crawl up my back, heavy
loaded on cheap narratives,
Gortari doubles, Atlantis sketched on Gorbachev's forehead:
you, yes, you, gator-mouthed agent—like gila progeny.
Let's hustle. Let's trade.
It is 1:27 A.M. in da rat Arctic.
What do i trade for with passion?

Language escapes me. Passion is smoke.
i dissolve.

It is in my nature to disappear. No sista', no brotha'.
No motha', no soul. This shred iciness is all,
a crazy register that destroys itself into Polaroid,
into a glacial sheet of multicolored border walls.

Let's foam & spin flamey
bluish tears for the Thing-Against-Itself, soul-less soul,
this film word surface. Sing out, baby.
Wobble & bop to town.

Drag yo' hands
across my fine-tuned work train named *Desastre*
en route to Freetown—engineered African shaman houses
smell of licorice, Ebola & famine blood, of hair torn,
of death owls & cancerous alcoholic livers, of babies sucking
this deep night to come,

then—a busted chink of afternoon copper light wakes us,
yo' sista' rolls in with a bag of lemons for Evil Eye,

for the seven inch ache in her abdomen.
Keep me in stride. You.

i am talking to you, fool. Don't
just sit there stretchin' yo' face.

Tell me why fire yearns for the heart.
Write it down. Say it. Fool. Speak the names.

Conjure the recitations from the coffee cup,
the steel-toe, border-crosser boots.

The grass rips up the morning snow lights, jagged & yellowish.
My AIDS face is hidden. Your rot, my epistemology.

i stand in pure light, a blaze of eyes & arms,
volcanic & solar, autistic, anti-written,
burned by mad friars & clerics, uptown
octupi readers, my long hair falls as reddish honey,
on a naked supple back,
        on breasts small & secretive.

Mystery evades me. Shadows crumble.
Without attention, i locate the love void & yet,
i know all is well. My blood rocks to a bolero
out of rhythm, a firefly's bolero that is,
the one in the dog eye. Hear me
warm up to the multi-night. Scribble poems &
        shout rebuke for the sake of scarred angels,
for Tara, who guides me
in her emeraldine, sequined night of lies.
Hear me now,

kin to the half collie language that i keep & walk.
Kin now, to the leaves that plunge to the floors;
swivel whiteness without axis, tectonic blasts
without mercy. Straightjackets float on the river infinity.

Pink-skinned fishes stare back
as they evolve into my shape, my babble stream
magnetic juan-foolery. Arm wrestle me
on the soccer lawn, kick me in the balls.
The murder music is for everyone.

        The Last Mayan Acid rock band
        plays Berlin's latest score:

dead trade market systems for the dead proletariats,
rip up from Bangkok to Tenejapa. Everyone is

meaningful & vomits, everyone deposits
a stench pail, into the Cube—

Neo-America,
without the fissure of intimate thighs. Cross over into fire,
hunger & spirit. i write on my hand:

the road cuts into a star. Go, now, go, fool.
In your lyric wetback saxophone, the one yo' mama left you,
the Thing-Against-Itself strapped across your hips.

Do not expect me
to name—this Thing-Against-Itself. Play it. Screw it.
Howl up to the Void, the great emptiness,
the original form.

Night Journal:
Keep on rockin', blues fish, in the gauze of the day into night. Out there
somewhere, Dis-America, pick up a chrome bone, the shards of the last Xmas
Presidential extravaganza. You, of course, fool.

Swivel into the clear. Float over the greenish migrant barracks pocked
with wire torsos, toes wiggle & predict our forthcoming delirium–
there is a velvet panther shouting out OM in funk, there is a tawny word
in the middle of the city thoroughfare, a planetary semi of lives slices
the wet animal in half. i am that punk half panther. My fierce skull &
mandible, formidable, my pelt is exact as witch quartz, a slashed leg
tumbles down the highway, battered by every dirty, steel wheel. Face up
to the sky, you, i said, to the brilliant gossip from the Goddess parade.
Outside, outside.

So.
Crawl up, baby, come on, keep on floatin'—
slidin', always: for black journeys, always in holiness.

blood on the wheel

blood on the wheel

Ezekiel saw the wheel,
way up in the middle of the air.
TRADITIONAL GOSPEL SONG

Blood on the night soil man en route to the country prison
Blood on the sullen chair, the one that holds you with its pleasure

Blood inside the quartz, the beauty watch, the eye of the guard
Blood on the slope of names & the tattoos hidden

Blood on the Virgin, behind the veils,
Behind—in the moon angel's gold oracle hair

> What blood is this, is it the blood of the worker rat?
> Is it the blood of the clone governor, the city maid?
> Why does it course in s's & z's?

Blood on the couch, made for viewing automobiles & face cream
Blood on the pin, this one going through you without any pain

Blood on the screen, the green torso queen of slavering hearts
Blood on the grandmother's wish, her tawdry stick of Texas

Blood on the daughter's breast who sews roses
Blood on the father, does anyone remember him, bluish?

> Blood from a kitchen fresco, in thick amber strokes
> Blood from the baby's right ear, from his ochre nose
> What blood is this?

Blood on the fender, in the sender's shoe, in his liquor sack
Blood on the street, call it Milagro Boulevard, Mercy Lanes #9
Blood on the alien, in the alligator jacket teen boy Juan

> There is blood, there, he says
> Blood here too, down here, she says
> Only blood, the Blood Mother sings

Blood driving miniature American queens stamped into rage
Blood driving rappers in Mercedes blackened & whitened in news
Blood driving the snare-eyed professor searching for her panties
Blood driving the championship husband bent in Extreme Unction

> Blood of the orphan weasel in heat, the Calvinist farmer in wheat
> Blood of the lettuce rebellion on the rise, the cannery worker's prize

Blood of the painted donkey forced into prostitute zebra,
Blood of the Tijuana tourist finally awake & forced into pimp sleep again

It is blood time, Sir Terminator says,
It is blood time, Sir Simpson winks,
It is blood time, Sir McVeigh weighs.

> Her nuclear blood watch soaked, will it dry?
> His whitish blood ring smoked, will it foam?
> My groin blood leather roped, will it marry?
> My wife's peasant blood spoked, will it ride again?

Blood in the tin, in the coffee bean, in the *maquila oración*
Blood in the language, in the wise text of the market sausage
Blood in the border web, the penal colony shed, in the bilingual yard

> Crow blood blues perched on nothingness again
> fly over my field, yellow-green & opal
> Dog blood crawl & swish through my sheets

Who will eat this speckled corn?
Who shall be born on this Wednesday war bed?

Blood in the acid theater, again, in the box office smash hit
Blood in the Corvette tank, in the crack talk crank below

Blood boat Navy blood glove Army ventricle Marines
in the cookie sex jar, camouflaged rape whalers
Roam & rumble, investigate my Mexican hoodlum blood

    Tiny blood behind my Cuban ear, wine colored & hushed
    Tiny blood in the death row tool, in the middle-aged corset
    Tiny blood sampler, tiny blood, you hush up again, so tiny

Blood in the Groove Shopping Center,
In blue Appalachia river, in Detroit harness spleen

Blood in the Groove Virus machine,
In low ocean tide, in Iowa soy bean

Blood in the Groove Lynch mob orchestra,
South of Herzegovina, south, I said

Blood marching for the Immigration Patrol, prized & arrogant
Blood spawning in the dawn break of African Blood Tribes, grimacing
& multiple—multiple, I said

Blood on the Macho Hat, the one used for proper genuflections
Blood on the faithful knee, the one readied for erotic negation
Blood on the willing nerve terminal, the one open for suicide

Blood at the age of seventeen
Blood at the age of one, dumped in a Greyhound bus

Blood mute & autistic & cauterized & smuggled Mayan
& burned in border smelter tar

       Could this be yours? Could this item belong to you?
       Could this ticket be what you ordered, could it?

Blood on the wheel, blood on the reel
Bronze dead gold & diamond deep. Blood be fast.

blood night café

Burials.
They come, they go.

Young boys with hard shadows on their girl faces
in the chrome box. The face goes with the knife in the coat pocket.
The knife goes with the gubernatorial tie on the screen.

Pick up dirt, make circles over
the fleshy mound of my palm. Stand like Travolta
hands in a flash, my white coat in a hula
wind cuts down over me. Breathe
old woman says to me. Spit.

Walk on
with Black spirituals inside.
Door slams on my tiny heart,
sirens come, go shoot lipstick

on Greyhound station windows.
My father strolls through the aisle,
a licorice cane, a Baptist ghost on fire.

abandoned blood

Gone to the drooler dungeon, the mother's buried kitchen, that is.
Gone to the steeple, precise, greenish, the father's abuse, that is.
Gone to the dog pelt infestation, the evening ruffled with sex, that is.
Gone to the taxi gypsy dressed in magic, the last glimpse of his thigh, that is.
Gone to the corporate xylophone jazz, the governor's pimp plantation, that is.
Gone to the pimple ruby girl clerkship, the fast daughter's suicide, that is.
Gone to the Greenback Queen of "C" Street, your aunt, the illegal, that is.
Gone to the half-moon, busted eye, the trunk orphan, smuggled, that is.
Gone to the lesson of Jew massacres, the sickle through your hair, that is.
Gone to the short viola, enchanted, the boy rape stuffed into the ear, that is.
Gone to the great emptiness, inside the ring, your last death, of course, that is.

blood suites

Chocolate ran to the store to fetch a quart of milk
got stuck bad, died on the floor.

Vanilla was wild about his new Camaro
when he got split upside the jaw.

Café stays home, clicks on the blue goddess
strolls to the stove to kiss *la navaja*.

say blood man

You telling me everything is all right,
the church in progress, the state in process
our army with ant noses, the forced potato
bridal cake without pubis, the altar smelter
this language in the sausage, this remedy
with razors, that is, with plutonium, this
atomic ventricle going into a rap about love
you know, the All, the Hood, the Rule, my
constant pouring urinal machine, astute
vested, armed to the lung, one nerve shows
your nipple dangle, shoo-bop, is that you
telling me, with your ripped mandible
at the newsstand stomping on a baseball
a bit of sugar, a wafer found on the way
you say, this cube little crystal theory
big bang from Kentucky beheaded, on the road
she was, you do say, she was, as always
inside a five-gallon jug, stuffed, the confession
in regalia, bluegrass anthems, the crime
sublime, dandy.

blood mouse manifesto

So, we come a full circle. Wait, I am first.
This hole, this personal vortex is mine.
Not the homicide Sphinx, the National Sphinx
is outside the hole, the Sphinx gets the cheese

> the provolone ass
> the mortadella gut
> the *salchicha* raisin eye
> the Thing-Against-Itself, the one
> on your nose, your reddish mandala
> from Fruit-Pick City, speckled
> a DNA aggression, against you.

No need for the *contratista* to slay your behind.
No need for the bully wine-maker grape king to haunt you.
No need. So the hole is.

Retain my epistemologically correct structures.
Say, fragrance, say, do-wop, say ribs on ice, say blue baby shouting
for *revolución*. A full circle, a weeping well,

mirrored
extravaganza of tiny pupils in search of honey,
a bun from the Goddess.

Call her, now. Call her. Say
Queen Tara, distiller of illusion
pray over me. May this hole
become a leaf on your dress.
Ten thousand branches, tiny prayers
tiny shivers. Ourselves
& others.

blood sockets

From my forebone to your name in Pimp Letters
from my acetabulum to your zebra cage,
the thigh camp where it roams.

From my front buck to your brain
from my spinal process to your taxidermy love affairs
from my candle heart to your devoted corporations in Korea
from my inner fibula to your love for my Japanese mother
from my island foot to your digital sperm prison

digital in its blue count of young men gone dry
digital in its factory trees where we hang the jaundice
digital in its reconstructed desires where we finger a devil
digital in its global suture ticktock of our existence.

blood gang call

Calling all tomato pickers, the ones wearing death frowns instead of jackets
Calling all orange & lemon carriers, come down the ladder to this hole
Calling all chile pepper sack humpers, you, yes, you the ones with a crucifix
Calling all garlic twisters caught in the winter spell of frozen sputum
Calling all apple tossers high up in the heaven of pesticides, stick faced
Calling all onion priests & onion nuns & onion saints killing for rain
Calling all tobacco pullers, thick leaf rollers in the ice burn of North Carolina
Calling all melon pitchers in the rivet machine, in the assembly bed of bones
Calling all artichoke pressers kneeling at the mount of signs chanting OM
Calling all peach slicers preserving shells in the form of a tiny orange fetus
Calling all lettuce skirts kicking lust down to the underworld soul prison
Calling all watermelon shiners paring the sugary womb in search of Goddess
Calling all cotton pilots seeding the froth on my mother's grave, rebellious
Calling all strawberry weavers threading your wire mesh heart with thorns
Calling all tomato pickers, the old ones, wearing frayed radiator masks.

blood from the native son

Remember me? Tijuana boy gone sour,
gone to the City Jeweler for luster? You, I said.

You left the red hammer with its face smashed.
You left the long coat of dust, a Hieronymus hat.
You left the viola between my tiny mother & you—
in flames.

You left the Baptist bible, the swiveling sperm flannel sheet.
You left the oxblood shoes cut & ruffled with extra heels.
You left the map to the Greyhound station, no ticket to Mercy.
You left the bastard poem, this blaze of Chihuahua inside my vest.
You left one shaving brush, one letter of desire in elegant writing.

I look to the trees for an embrace,
gaze at the darkness eating the bark.

When the moon comes up, I touch the pock marks
black chalk, the solar winds.

blood tysons

Black fist will come burning & you will contemplate the oceans
thunder panther will strike your street & you will think of autumn
blue dancer in sickles will crash at your station & you will ask for air
Harlem woman will drift from your shirt & you will deny her
John Razor will cut into your heart, a wreck molecule & you will laugh
Sita, your lover's thighs will leave convulsions & you will keep on
writing

you will keep on writing
about forest water, how it reels
how the briefcase you carry
electric & loud with fast strangers
& you will contemplate

the late office night, the window half open
square lights in the distance, figures
perhaps a face, a magnetic arc
devilish, violet blossoms,
against the window, inside
                        your night.

2pac blood

Be right in the pool cue shot
Be right in the night swoon hit
Be right in the swamp leaf kiss

Be right in the tattoo sting
Be right in the alley fur
Be right in the tiny eye

Be right in the bone blast shoe
Be right in the lung rose drop
Be right in the crimson site mark
Be right in the broken wall talk

Be right in the stutter dog
Be right in the mother death
Be right in the father club
Be right in the singular sky
Be right in the statement laid
Be right in the march upside

Be right in the word light
Be right in the word light
Be right in the word light

aztec blood sample

Where is the goddess, Tara, now, crack open my chest?
Where is the healer woman, La Catalina, your robe in green hallucinations?
Where is the obsidian point, Mexico—the road to the abyss?

chicken blood townships

Say, fool. Cut the shit, all right. Your fancy ass lingo.
Get it? Cut it. Just smack the chicken wing off your table.
Haul the dead mop through this national factory floor.
The heads you say? You say they remind you of your
red ancestors, the glue from the ligament you say
this see-through sour reminds you of holiness,
& the pelt, the fawn-colored skin rummage, you say
must be your land occupation, the bone of course, fool
the main bone, cut through the back across the rump
you say, this is your beginning, your Creation Story
it's all on your apron, fool, the continent ejaculations,
the gizzard deportations, *el buche*, say it, *el buche*
your gizzard neck—boy, that what I call the knowledge.

blood fourteen

Stranger come to meet you in the shade, in full regalia.
Come to greet your bosom, your flint, last breath at seven.
Full definition this side of the black bark. Light kills light
for a moment, then we swim into the eternal. You, for
example, with the jacket noose, the hot wire of redemption
caught on the leg, the·shrapnel inside the thigh, this amber
spit going down effortlessly, this mock love on 14th Street.

ezekiel's blood

As I was saying. Before you startled me with your perfume.
Rather, with your ancient Indian mother, rather—with the split
this hollowness inside. Inside what, fool? You want to know
inside what fool? Dig in & be merry.

There was a castle once
built beneath the earth.
You could call it a dungeon.
You could call it a desire.
You could even call it a march toward death.
You could even say we were on that road. You, fool.
& me. We were.

& in that darkness, the bright angel of the eye.
In that burial we found each other. We picked up
the bones, the shame caskets. Your name especially.
I heard the voices. Your little mother, your little father
telling stories of Cain & Abel. There was an eye
in the center of the pit.

The eye saw all light. The eye saw all murders.
The eyes spoke the way eyes speak. No possibility.
No Loving. Until the eye left its burning accents.

sugarman's blood (yeah, you)

Say, sugarman—yeah, you, behind the filling station
shuffling under the seat, come on up & stare a little
come on, pull out the jute pack stuffed with your mother
& her oranges, come on now, pull back the handkerchief
tied around your neck, to one side, turquoise, elegant campesino
walk this way, down the aisle, huddle up to the corner
lay down your soaked hands, your tobacco coat in smoke
it is time to rest your head bobbing to one side
toward the perfume. Select, bring your ancestors from Rwanda
call them up from Atzcapolzalco & Acaponeta, door
is open. Lay down & swim on the weasel oil, this
butcher paper negligee, this oceanic thunderbolt, your
antelope carcass, haul it in & deliver the fur shank
your cut legs, torso nerve shawl ribbons, let's make
a wreath, it is appropriate for your people, now show
the pancreas, as an autonomous continent, sunken
& the liver, sequined in whiskey & void, toss it up
to this wicker throne, come on sugarman blue, the prize.

last blood words

In the mind,
in the mind pig, we say—World.
In the forearm, in the swing of things—Property.
In the eye, in the center of the obsidian—Art
(excuse me, did he capitalize art?)
In the rib, the last bastion of patriarchy—Heritage.
In the hand, the free one, we say—Love.
In the belly, let us say—Universe.
In the noose knot, outside, in the externals—Destiny, add Nation
(did he add it correctly?)
In the moon separating itself from the clouds—Goddess or Will
(or the moon separating itself from the clouds?)

queen blood america

Took her to the basement did you, fool?
Twine your lust fast around the neck
in the Manroom of resentments.

You poured there, you pulled the face off
did you? Now the town hunts you—
the innocent ones snap the ulna & aim
for your spine. Your ransom notes light up
our town square. Year after year, you
bring down your torch, Herzegovina
Kasakhstan, Denver—the one you stole
from us. A silly child century floats

above you.
See how elegant she is, in her torn
sequined gown of perfect lights—see
the doubled-up shape of this fixed body,
how we walked her to your side—
the doubled-up shape of this fixed body.

my rice queens

my rice queens

You drag it across Tijuana, drag it hard from Tecate
make sure the face remains elongated & oval, translucent,
light to the touch, docile—the key: whitish with the eyes
upwards, yellow to the ragged hills where one day it will return.
You the King: you the tiger speaks the long grain hump, hear
it sing to you, with a crooked guitar, wine-colored string
throat, You the Baby. First you drag it, then you turn the tiny
head back, make it eat wire, enter the wire, the barbed scar blackness,
you turn the tiny head. This is the lesson,
you see, this is the way revealed for the first time.
Flip you, it speaks. Flip me, baby—burn it deep with glass
high-class brass, a sliver of dead Mexico so it may dream
as all rice-boys dream, burnt orange-face rice-boys with
or without the flame sweetness that comes later. Hear me
again with or without the fire hustle underground
like tuber root, like blue stream jazz, rip it up until you shoot
the flower in the mud, in the groin, upside the alleyway.
Dr. Coyote knows. Oh, yes, he does. Night Chevy Man
picker of the Red Rice People. Weep here, the signs say
to the rice. Weep, here, the light says to the Street
Rice Queen. Weep, here again raps
the Rice Killer in search of another wise throat. Betwixt
two radish heavens, alongside the bristled fans of the sugar beet.
There, on that road—so far from Tijuana Drive, the sack
listens to you. Ready, I say. I am ready *Señor, sí señora*.
Jump, border spike. Take me first, the Rice *Llorona* says.
You took me yesterday. Take me today.

this is the z

Z for elongated suffering cheese wheel
rodent dweller seeking wisdom in the fold of the blue
little letters that can be tricked to read all
da freedom in the universe. Except the rodent
has a hard time gettin' to the center since it
cannot distinguish between the margin & the heart
hunger & enlightenment.

border-lovin' & sinister

for Joshua Ryan

Aside from the sawed can through the face,
I strut with my ass high off the ground, I saunter
to the beat of Morrison & his dead-eye babies
from the sixties. Syrup vaginas & basted
screwed garlic cocks. How we waited for fire
to weep & stone trumpets to howl. To kiss.
So, who's famous now, without them? The border
girl that dreams of being a Guard-slayer comes
often. We drink & make ourselves reddish
with bitter notes & wild with our lonely knives.

**one thousand strings of oblivion
& a bucket of grave dirt**

Kasakhstan rises from the Communist rubble.
I suck the ant from my mustache &
wonder if my mother appears before me.
Is that you behind the curled sage? The burn
inside my ear locket? My Turkish skirt, green
my little playthings—that you left. El Paso
waves behind you, falls apart in the rearview.
Go singing. Go standing, against me.

a banjo you left unbridled with rage

As always, I carry your star, embroidered. Over
my heart—this plenum & plain universe.
My net bag is empty. I keep it empty & hollow-eyed.
The cut shoes are ashes. This tiny nail, classical
in its abandonment helps me police the night. We
sit & count the sky rivers. Inside the clouds

there are wild forests, split oceans
a son's paw, striped & broken. Hear them unfurl.
Recognize me, now. Recognize me, now?

a bee head rests on my shoulder

A silver tourniquet for a tie, two eggs of slaughter
one feminine tibia of Kantian certitude. Insects,
priests wet your lips with me. The bread before us
reminds me of the last century. Webbed coats
& light-colored brassieres, a novel left unread.
Nobody knocks for you, fool. The floor dips over
the moon & scatters my bed. In the fog banks
my longish hair, my honeycombs.

this semi-skull worker

To rotate away from the Guard, to flee
with sandals & a whistle in the night.
This is the skull worker's wish.

To tear & deepen the bearded shadows.
Unshaven, look up to the bulb, charred
in the tarred barracks. I scratch my legs.
My hands in the pocket. The face glistens
from the steel that hangs on the high wall. Rock
me with morphine, busted—lungs open
speckled & negative.

the blue-eyed mambo that unveils my lover's belly

Come down to the violin-colored table
walk up to her frenzy, the bracelet she wears.
Brush her ear with your lips & leave.
When the cymbal strikes, fall with your arms
open & fly next to her. Over her translucence,
the frayed blouse, razored & stiff. The flame
she murders with her teeth, this small stone
this hand that you offer. To her, to her
you say, you—the one under the phosphor.

blues pack last mile

And they want me to believe. Give me,
they say—your tainted shadow. The jelly
coin come down from your dead eye. Now mop
it, they say. Bring me up towards the half-lit
gas station. I dream the gasoline, see
me take the multi-colored ghosts to my lips.
Wake me in the vat, the double boot patrols.
So, I give it to them—this wavy blood spirit.

selena in corpus christi lacquer red

In my own Tex-Mex breakdown, suffix
for eternity—I dash to the bottom, refrigerations;
what I could not have, gone white. Come up
with the harmonica for wings. Blow
the G, then strum my ancient brain, in a French hotel.
Blues & Rancheras, tombs, S with an X on her back.
You taste the Goddess, now—Quiet. Me:
in the ashen flower, upright, proud in your rising blood.
Moody & swollen in da cabaret, naked. Grip
me, in the mud, in sudden flame, red
star in Corpus Christi lacquer—going down, maguey milk
into an odd-angled branching needle, a howl Virgin—
the one I wanted to deliver me. Open me, X-Selena
w/your vocal & bruised accordion breast.

pick up your severed head & let me get on, baby

Been standing—since '56. In the shame light,
in the blues riff apology clinic. For the ticket
North, oh, yeah this what they told me
at the station. Been leaning hard on the Mount,
asking for brownness, I mean a true brownness halter
not this decay river, sliding to a copper rash.
Not this
kicked-in rubber cheek. Haa! Just do me
this last favor, baby. You see that torso, grass
splayed vein boy, so buoyant, see him? In
his tiny form; this is how he loves to appear,
see? Protection's like gold, he says. Take a look,
knock him down to the shanty bar, where
he will transform, but first. Baby, I said it once.
Pick up your severed head &
                                I'll pick up mine.

explode this letter w/ this

X is for fancy tacos sold w/ Mayan Rebellion
J is for the first White God initially meant for burial in Juárez.
Was it the Mexican Revolution? Was it? Haaa!
Fooled you—sucker in red striped despair pajamas.
Where was you?

J is for never enter the Nirvana Joke Tree.
T is simple. Ten gloves will mark your dishes, in eternal
service boy, jackal. The bean dish is familiar isn't it?
The fruit pie, calabash sweet tomato is foreign since
you have been away so long in Tamerica. Tuber
is simple too. Mash chest. Mash eyes. Mash foot.
Then you fry. You pour hottish, sugar chunk boot
so mellow bite it. You never learn. Sit there then,
wait for the trolley to take-take you: up *Maquila* Road,
swerve in vomit, pay stub to Food Mountain.
Square off & blow your cigar nose. Move, baby
move move.

edward hopper visits my el paso soul

Say, Hopper, stick around. Paint my nipples
reddish & ochre yellow against the flat sea.
This way, with a greenish chaser, a flicker
steadfast. Two souls in the silvery groove boat.
Bend the brush to Deportation, the princess etched
on my left arm. This sequin flesh I call my voice
speaks to you. Kiss Juárez, I say. In the beehive
markets. Loosen my head & foggy eyes roll up.
She-skirts & torn tortillas. Vinegar for
the little girl stealing bread; this is her lesson.
Bring me up, next to the piano bar, shine
my face umber, my soap back wild: driving &
humble, perfumed in the sky gauze. Shave me, yes.
My armor waits. So kind. Next to the wool
barbershop stool, hang it.

border-crosser with a lamborghini dream

for A. Hedge Coke

A temptation limo? Here:
sturdy, so Mexican in the Indian
light, he could swing his arm up for air, for honey
in the cup he jumps. High heaven Jute-Boy, hey,
listen up &

stop the horseshit. Climb down the sugar pile.
Bop & screw the head on gently. Fix the gizzard.
Annihilate the bass progressions, the ones
you make with your suffering. Mind me, now.
Now stick the floor, in bone shoe. Swish the ulna.
Chop the baskets for a pesticide sideshow. Ready?
Come on fool. Are you ready or not? Is that you
peeling the jelly scarf? Are you serious,
in this shade, tonight? Across Mesquite, out
where the kerosene & human stacks smoke,
keep on hummin'.

swish guitar for the abused federations

Hey, kid—wadda I say? Say, sit, boy fool. You sit
or blam. Now, get this: I said P is for ask me once again
in the mattress, red striped cup where you weep.
Tell me about your tiny Bosnia, pubis, your little
Mayan ass. Come on now—repeat after me. Q
is for the shade your mother left you, for a high
heaven lawyer. Who's gonna take care of you now?
At the crossroads, that's it. Pick up
the severed gut, some shriveled cat paw. Tuck it in,
bop to town & blow: your innocent certitude, your tawny
lips so full, so much in love. Better be you.

slashed epistemology & wire cutters

Fry my eggs green. Cure the insanity in my shoes.
Offer St. Jude candles for rain & democracy.
Weave a black shawl on April Fools', to fool who?
Glance with your dead eye at the cheese wheel,
golden in its thigh form, in its bountiful breast.
Toss up the sugary wafer, in Tamerica, in this sod.
Jump Jute-Man, blast mariachi, howl in a beggar whisper.
Crash against the amber tilt house, full of bolts
no doors no screws.

jute-boy at the naturalization derby

In the Chevy-sack, mottled & sharp: lean boy, to the ride.
Did you draw out your Hoo-Doo literature, the bone-for-itself?
Remember the riff bone, the one from the goddess-shank?
& the giraffe frame, the self-portrait, longing & philosophical—
was that you, in Low Tucson, hoisting another flame?
Stole it? You did. In your reflex for passion, in your arsonist
lazy fourth eye, the one next to the ear.

Eye # 1: for the Jute Border tragedies, so buoyant:
> *this is how you measured your exile, nervous & joyous.*
Eye #2: for the Ocelot cut man you smuggled into your existence:
> *this is how you rose up & struck down your torturers.*
Eye #3: for the drowsy leaf eater, so polite in his self-abuse:
> *this is how you returned, to your tiny womb voice—victorious.*
Eye #4: this da Rice Warrior, can't see, but it there:
> *O, this—your language, in gestation; the last flight*
> *shoot up, from your raw Motherland.*

We note
your animal laboratory: one treasured police dog leg, sprawled
one parakeet vest, two coyote tracks—to cover up your migrant
tardiness into bone-being. How you raced the tyrants, their feathers
& spelled forgiveness, then genocide. But, the enemy stands
before you. Can you identify? Let's leave the question
open.

gestapo bowls on the plank

He pours his soul, his
sour porridge in mash. Rise up w/ the buttons, you.
Hey—fool, you. With clown stripes & seersucker
pants. Yeah, you goof boy with matted hair. Let's
drink to the beat of a *maraca*. Inside my head, America
the bead drops & rolls a tiny awakening. To transform, to
reorganize the septum of Slave. Haaa-haa, I lied.
Clean the bowl, mark the trash, honor your rebellion.

from an extinct ukraine, i sing

Jab da jute bag, haaa! In my revolution re-verb,
this uncanny ferocity I acquired from slaveries, underground.
So many days in solitary,

international & ancient holes,
so, I says, so—as I spit through the winged groove.

Tight was the rap, the casket my Hoo-Doo God fixed. His crucifix.
& basted in basement ash & mute light from his youngest son:

O, Count Poet that prays for discovery. I laugh
with my swollen mouth, my heavy hands, thumbs up, ringing.

Two rice stars burn across my chest. Poland & Chiapas in my vest
liquid—see? Glow baby, Mexican bluish.

My first source was iron: this wavy lookout point, tear duct.
A compass, betwixt the nail

& the cross, phosphor boulevards,
one angel for steadfastness & explosion. O, yes,

Explosion, my favorite sister—Axe, I call her, say Axe, give
me some smoke, make me; I giggle again, in my carcass boots.

broadway indian

wixárika

          What
did I know?

Tepic—Nayarit,
 Ixtlán,

Ixcuintla. Where was I?
The Huichol smoke.

        Coras
      in Bogart
hats awaiting blessings from Big Al to hand them agricultural prowess, a drop
of chemical awareness into a new form of capitalism. This?

Or was my   Tepehuano
sister in
a shawl draped

       with rain the answer?
    Shawl rain on the concrete—sex kicks

        & belly abuse? Madonnas
        as always,

as bequeathed
from slave time, from Cortés

& his Spanish cock clergy. But
this

was not Ixtlán or Tepic. This
was a Mexican assemblage
                    awaiting to reincarnate into Barbra Streisand on
    Columbus Street in San Francisco,

next to the stripper machines. This was my lost agriculture
in neon flesh, in fresh   wetness.

strip / from chinatown

Walk the arid strip

from   Chinatown

wondering about my dead mother
Lucía. I go back.

The fat hand of priests
& *ganadero* ranchers

who rent land to the poor
Indian blasted with five century pieces

                    come together after a few drinks from Spec's
tavern. It isn't Tepic.

Is it?
Amado Nervo Boulevard with
the face of Dolores del Río,

        the silver screen queen w/ a Catholic

penchant toward self-erasure & Indian rage.
                    Amado Nervo. I think on the term

—Amado.

                                    Indian rage?
                                    Chicle children,
a prayer

at the bottom of the sugar cane day,
at the *Instituto Nacional Indigenista*—our overlord,
                                                   our conversion machine. This

is how I walk,

in this gait.
I am going for an Italian dish. Further than last time.

Scribble on the napkin.   Draw a circle,   then a square.
                                 Two eyes mesh into the triangle of love, dream
& magic.

The chicle
woman comes at me

in Spandex & fishlace.   In black breasts.

This is America

she tells me—a forlorn
& toothless smirk, with her skirt torn

& her shirt on my face.   You are a Ladino.
                                      A Ladino poet.

He
who
writes
his skin

against his skin. Monkey skin,
tortuga. Breathe

she tells me. Breathe & you

    shall be free from this capitalist yoga.
                Scrape your music off my shoes &   be free.

subzero

What did I know?

                         Except this subzero. This
vortex-spirit warp
soprano

voice as I strolled with expectations for a Bengali poet soul somewhere at the
end of the asphalt tunnel. An actress in heat, Tatéi? Stabbed with *duende*, her
ankles tapping on my small wedge-table,

haunting me
into an erotic iambic. Vortex ghost lover boy

is this what you wanted?
                         Is this

                                                what you wanted?

Is this the color? Is this the proper language?
Is this your sub-dream,

your sub-opening again
                   coming up asking for night
                   air
in this city nation? Please

free your hands from mine she tells me.
                         She denies she is Indian.
                         So do I.

Hey, bro' take this *finca* off my back. Hey, bro' take this journey chakira bead collar sold for five thousand pesos away. Gather your own prophecies, your own rain, your own sexual powders. Lake Chapala glows ahead of me, near Chinatown.   I was born there. In these pesticides &

slashed neon hulas.
Can I walk with you?

Can I rumble up

your sleeve into your tiny desires,
she asks. Was it me?

No.

I say. No, it wasn't you.
Alone, the both of us.
                    She wears an Ékatewári shawl,
                    the one that protects you
from the Evil Wind,
the one that sounds like
        violins

descending a Grant Street basement staircase,
crackle & spit & crack & flow
                into your veins   with a sky feeling. So

vast you ask for air only.

I did not hear you   she says. Tatéi

or Dolores? Streisand?

She doesn't see me come leaning.
Doesn't
sense

my *ranchero* face break at the edge of Río Santiago,
next to *la ranchería*

               where we trade for a crossing, a dug-out canoe to
        carry us across

into the Mestizo side.
I am listening to a Mexican transistor radio

       next to her.   Dotted in her dress.   Dotted

       in her alien   faces   as I slouch toward her tiny mirror.

I wander with embers, these dry partners
        with drunk rings   outside the burger

corporation shop, you know the one you always

visit. Next
to Grandfather Fire to be exact. Where we part our   poems,

talk sex & coffee & scars & timelessness
         with a bit of mercy, this time, just a   bit. Grandfather

Fire. He listens.

My advisor

is orange & red & black & green outline flesh.
Tatewarí,

Grandfather.

I bow & circle you. He listens.

     How could I contain all   this? Could

it all fit into the sly American grooves I have carved for myself,
     after Tijuana, after dead   Mexico? After

     Sonora

& its red tin buses, broken open
with chickens & splayed starfish

with me   & my brothers, sisters   angled
     for sweetness in its combined tubing?

A red tarp

     in the back: Sonora
     in   desolation, where

I sat crouched

with the night   ticket, going   to *El Norte*.

     Sell & trade. *Indio*

     they said.

     You'll never make it, give me your rings
     & I'll take you, the *chofer* said. So

I step into the bananas,   in the back,   into

         the mounds of mango,
                    plantain
                         & jalapeños. The *verdulero*

told me to dig deep

& everything is going to be all right.

It was you

standing next to the water bucket behind the mule-boy, she says

& I am talking to her on Columbus,
a worker sex woman
teen

         image
         mirage
         Indian
         myself
         reversed
         behind
         the mule,
         up
         ahead
         of me,
         next
         to
         the

lonely
scraped
shadow
at
the
curb,
fast
soaked
in
thigh
glamour,
inserted
so
faithfully
into
the
mountain
edge
of
chrome

cars.

                              If
                              I

                 could cruise. If I

                 could   step

& drive

across the wires. If   only.   If

    only—

       that is all I know, If onlys. With
       my deer-horn   sombrero.

Carved

& swinging my hair, blackish & full of lights,

    a dream form from above,

from Great
Grandfather Blue   Deer,
       Kauyumári. He listens too.

He gives me advice. This year

      he says the   corn will fall early,

    at the center of the *milpa* you

    will find a ball of smoke,
    the hair

in a strange smudge of earth & worms,

        you must
        kneel   there, toss

flowers   climb back

up

to
 your
pueblo, go,

tell them this year the corn will be small & you will have to travel
north again,

                        speak about your people, so
                        that you may find beauty

& speak of beauty. Live
in beauty   this is your destiny,

            beauty in the rough cut of stone,

        mosquito
        & gray *finca* water as it closes

        into your   trembling   village.

                        Under

                        Big Al's
                        plastic

canopy, his own steeple of fast

eyes
& thick hands—there I pray. Near Columbus Street,

                                    inside
                                    Kaliwey, my
temple, twig tower
on the inside slope of my village—where I go chattering.

        Outside   the flavor of *nixtamal*,

   corn slush softened
        with stones & woman hands, it comes to me,

        rolled
        & speckled with trapezoids of burnt food &

        ash.

I kneel

            again

            with a little enamel plate of beans

        for Tatéi Werika Wimari,

    our Corn Goddess, she is here

                        above me, in the Kaliwey, I
hold her up   somehow,
wherever I go.

From military blast,   from *ranchero* greed,
          from medical supply helicopter pilots,

from *promotor* bilingual teacher
on the mountain come smiling

with books   about the *Presidente's* new program for

us,
to change,
to change
they keep saying   —to change.

kaliwey

In the Kaliwey,

blood   enamel.

In

saucepan, I cut the chicken's head off,

as I pray & hold up my hands to the table,
small, thick yellow tortillas, too. On the ground:

this is my table,   on the shadow
of green, yellow sparkles, coffee—

colored hands, the essential plants.
Liberate us, I cry. From misery, into the blue void,

into the upward pyramid-shaped

abyss

where Kauyumári descends   light &   words,

into this Great Emptiness. Advise

me by the dawn hummingbird flocks.
Near Chinatown, by the Janis Joplin

poster   black lights. By Jimi

      Hendrix & his bulbous hair,

      barefoot.

      You are the Great Hunter, they told me,
      the bent propagator of green howl—of

      Mexican blue suffering.

From the mix of safari hats, voices & kitchenware,
by the Vietnamese

      tailor shop, up a few blocks,
      Grandfather Fire calls me,

      he reminds me of my mission, my   inner

      prowl speaks,

            hidden almost,

            from the traffic glare,
            from Ladino

            town   fright.

tatéi

Upside my arms, the shadow of my dream crawls toward the sky.
The blackish tan coat, the pipe stem; all this & the wrinkled neon lips, Big Al
comes to me, in his hawk loneliness from the escape ladders of the sex
dancers, one ancient poet from Duluoz, the other from Chihuahua with
fingers for bullets & a cotton shirt for power: the arsenic tufts of Tipeyote for
a heart. Dotted at the four corners, He comes down, perfumed. I lay with my
lover, my shadow. Tatéi

      Tatéi, I call her. This time

          Tatéi of the Pointed
          Ocean Tongue.   Cross-legged

      with descriptions of this scene gone down in silk ties & smoke,
remembrance & quiet fire.

Can I love?

        This is the question

   every

Indian carries in the sage locket. She asks me.

      Can I love enough to cry out my soul, enough to
hack off the moon, as my ancient mother Lucía used to say—her pointed
voice still calls me too: the ocean-sequined night that kisses my skull.

69

I huddle

       the impossible river

       toward the bay, then

       I stall &

stay suspended,

           before the avalanche,   before

the next question from the sub-world.

     I crumble in burlap &
     suck up the tendrils

   from Jack

   the clairvoyant holler poet,   at the curb. Can

        he see me? See him, clutched
        & aching, roman & elegant,
        ·with a vapor & gasoline-flickered vest.

Before the unbrave machine.

We stand & ooze & riff

& groove into Al's porno shop Queenscape.

Morphined   into the outer edge again.

Hey, I say,

hey   give me

some aloe so I can smudge the bridge,

the pocked angelic timelessness that sneaks

across my breast bone.

I huddle

& wander into another language,

to anaconda swivel street beats,
the blurred rush before us all. I wait for a little man

to cross as he crushes another cigarette in

Chinatown.

I want to undo the round prison,

this stony slime, this air of city solitude

& plantation euphoria. I am not alone.

The Goddess   keeps me active
in her fragrant green robes, her shrine-stop amber.

Tatéi, I call. Tatéi.

My marigold,
I am calling you   too.
My fenced-in
melancholy,
another quasi-birth
toward innocence,
that is all: always toward
—a shiver? In

                    the connections of music, bird wing,
            flatboard offerings, corn gruel &
                    deportation,   drunk statuettes,
                    gilded & sewn into my pant cuffs,
        -   hummingbird designs;   all   asking
                    for more air. For clouds.

Woodpiles & bleedings left by my father. That is all I own. Talk to him now
by the Xiriki, this asphalt flatboard where I waver   inside the plank candles
& bowls, the ones used for cleanliness by the *Mayordomo*. Become a crystal,
my almond-eyed, Mystery-maker whispers.

Become a crystal

—the goal,

the eye

in the center strip,   by the greenish bedrooms & bathhouses

                    where you wept
                    & shaved before a shred mirror on the way
to an Indian grave, unmarked. Unknown. Untied.

Filled with newspapers,
deerskin & wet cigarettes,
sleepless. Frozen—
dead about the century, hunched
next to the millions of Wixárika's confined
in rubble, unshaved: unwrapped
& broken fibulas, inserted
through the brain, pubis,
the colony of trench coat
lamp chests with phosphor
eye buttons, a   rose
still stands alone
there—where   you fall.   -

Become a crystal, Tatéi whispers

as I drag a drink into my mouth,   on this wide blend of stripes,
colored glass & cold legs. Jump to the night Jute Indian band, the loco
plastic stomp. Bust back

to the top grade where the other
dwellers live, in fullness & antibiotic readiness
for the next monkey virus cutting across the Congo, then

Helsinki, then

the new Prague Cafe, the one where Big
Al sends his best customers.

    To kiss my dead father's feet, to   embrace his old bones,
   to lift up the tiny Huichol-colored yarn crucifix, my mother knotted
into his crossed hands,

       to sing, maybe to sing outside   with bent music,
       rolling in the fog banks of the village, a few hours,
       down the city mountain—the Santiago   River appears.

border wire / spina

Border wire

& more pesticides

in drum vats, in Ford

& General Electric,   in assembly tubing, in   hemorrhage skirts,
in industrial openings across Matamoros to Tijuana, American

                                                    Electric

on both sides,

          the Santiago crashes into ammonium,

into chlorofluorocarbon   fountains, into wood varnish

& black fingernail

hieroglyphs,   into spina bifida,

          into seven
                    babies
                    with one

head without
        a brain,
the shape of a broom,
a mop of snails. I stop

      & lean & cry,   again.

      My father's confident ragged

ghost

      waits at the stop light. He says, come down.
      Come & let's go now,

      he says. Let's go now to the second twin mountain, he says,

the one where   you   were born.

stroke this locket scar

Now,   by the river—I raise my hand   to my ear.
       I stroke the locket scar, the root,
       the hair hash & the fuse. The vapor

     & the glass, I stroke, the inside opening,

     the red wetness,

     fiber stream

     in the shape of a harmonica,

                 I blow the notes.

                 Play my brain,

                 (in Paris)

                 a French hotel, leaking with juice,

     sex water brine   bath powders,
     my head,

     severed, with a gaping   lip across my forehead.

           In the river.   I gaze.

(This   is   who I am?)   Son

of General Electric. My mother hemorrhaging again
at the sweatshop steel

pool hall glamour

next to the assembly levers, the phosphor pulleys,
the leather & wire from the grilled engine.

                      This is who I am? Son

of Ford plantations in Hermosillo. Indian sputum drooled
from an arsenic vat meant for foreign semi-conductors.

      Maquila John, they   call me,

      Hey

      Broadway, Big Al shouts, hey   Broadway,

      now

      doncha
      tell me
      you just
      found out
      how you
      got to
      where you
      are at?

kauyumári, i sing to you

Kauyumári, I sing to you, sacred deer advisor, to you alone, besides my father, besides Tatéi, besides the village in ashen flower roof, I sing to you, beside Tatéi in Spandex & Big Al, *El Mayordomo*. Walk me to the living, to their soft-ended feet & leave me there, incandescent in your bluish maize pelt, before I become an orphan, in America—on this side, before I divide into light & neon, in the Kaliwey prayer house of the forgotten hope-shoe makers. Take me to their fragrance once again, to their corn fingers & stone bowls of mash chili paste, to peasant longing, back & forth; suck me back into the universe.

William Carlos,

        a young, black poet, blows
    Puerto Rican poems across my chest

& I rise.

     The Santiago   swivels

     across the corner, tosses

         & swishes its Japanese   skirt,

     across strapped coffee cans
     for offerings, blind man pencils. I

rise

as my father appears whistling. He shuffles his feet

as he used to,   he   burns the strap

across his forehead & his net bag is full of thistle,
new corn & ocotillo.

He whistles as he used to, a melody from Cheyenne,
Wyoming, where he learned about snow in the early 1900s,

he quotes the hair & wood drum,
he points to the lean
windmills behind me.

He says they are handsome, naked & hungry.

Willy Carlos

blares his Puerto Rican poems about the latest new Latino dance craze.
First,

you throw your head back twice, he says.
Let's talk about the new Mexican revolution, he sings.
I want to say Sarajevo, I want to say this is my Ukraine
& spit at the hydrant where my sisters sleep & drink
their street news & fathom the elixir come rolling
from the ragged hills.

Weave it, he says.

Weave in   your bright lines,

the ones shooting from your belly,

weave it there

                in acid streams, come now,

                                for two thousand

                pesos, weave it hard
                against the brash light, the chrome
                melting cars as they pass you by,

 as you   wander. Weave it
        into your anthem, the one every poet is reciting right now,
across the piers,
        strangled or alive, jumping from on high, in shredded
blues dresses.

Remember Lucía, he asks me, remember   her?

Lucía,
in Chinatown produce markets. Radish & perch baskets,
oranges & rice bowl Lucía. Stand still so she can see you. Scroll down from
your patched apartment, abandoned in ancestor stones, bright, clockwise, one
hand waving

        the other   hushed.
        Come down from the mountain, from Maquila Road.
        Illuminate & pour into this city, this

sub-ground.

Lucía & Willy   in the subway. Beneath.

She paints

            a self-portrait
of giving & seeing & healing & dying. Legs veined, wavy,

        her tiny breast bones. Lucía comes down

        her striated monastery of blown glass & straw,
        maize   with split eyes,

            red & gold teeth,

            saffron. I crawl to her,

    in this rain street of Indian initiations, on the Mount.

        She comes to me from the flophouse pinnacles,
        still   living in a whirled, reddish gown,

        a gentle & tragic touch against the waning sunlight,
        a bird next to the embers—the Italian deli, blackish too,

        not asking, not speaking, not saying.
Not speaking.

Each incarnation is different: William Carlos blows into my ear,

he throws his head back twice & plays a mambo beat with his fingers.
He speaks about the fog in the Boulevard of Lost Souls, how it sings of
youth, he says my mother looks for me at times, in   ocean boats
among aged fishers, but Tatéi consoles me, now
in   the shape of a dove.

12,000,000 Indians, maybe

        8,000,000. Paste little mirrors in the bluish haze,
                in the mountain prisms of Universal Maquila America,
Inc. We

        all look up at midday to shake the light of Tayaupá,
                our Sun Father.

Our Father Sun   on Broadway, how

he heals Big Al's wounds & Big Al doesn't know. I twist
my shoulders & suspect Willy is right, as he leaves.

        Each life is different. He says. But not in

        the sub-void, not in   this

        rouge & infinite Low Universe. Butchered

across time & loss & eternity. Across Mexico, dead,

with a string of dried hummingbird rulers
in a flask of vinegar & jerez cheap fruit wine.

The Hope-shoe   makers
                                                       know.

In the throng of nervous & vomiting escalators, peasant twine & tight
fitting paper tuxedos. Bursting with desert songs, unscathed. The throng rolls,
long & greenish, in its own mix down of jazz worship & war longings,
across charred lamps, polished green Ducati bikes—O yes, there are stars up
there, a syrup of stars in a Caruso Arc of Triumph, milk cartons glow at the
curb, tiny poets with the arms of Venus de Milo, with the voice of corn sha-
mans in search of the Dove Words, throng music comes down, silly & trium-
phant, opal & sweat,   my sliding heart,
              in this flash

of death, agency & cosmos.

              Lucía

stands tall. She reminds me of Tatéi,   flickered & stained & in topaz &
emeraldine bracelets from a trinket shop   on the way to the
mountain village. Thin hands to the side, still & liquid.

Ten million years Lucía will be standing there, at the deep of the sierra. They
will come down from *El Picacho*, her village & celebrate, barefoot & in a
circle dance   as Grandfather hollers

the story

of the Beginning,

as he speaks to the New Sun. Stare

into the morning fire & you will see. Famine

so much famine & so little

magic.

What did I know? Tepic—Nayarit,

Ixtlán, Ixcuintla. Where
was I?   The Huichol smoke.

Coras in Bogart hats

awaiting blessings from Big Al

to hand them agricultural prowess,

a drop of chemical
awareness into a new form of Capitalism.

diaspora. night.

The bass voice of the   neon   worm
above me knows: calls out
about the fall of the earth, oil & hydroelectric rape. Machine boys &
machine girls, with their long rivet arms, legs crossed, weaving & spitting.
Clocking & timing,

                                    folding & washing, serving &
pulling, wrapping & boxing, packing & dipping, acid & fumes, blood &
corn.

A drag Queen from Finnochio's passes by.

        Her hands dissolve, boil   & sweat in my

                                    Diaspora. Night.

My father, the elder, steps up, the deer-horn shapes above him, below him
the tambourine, under Big Al, under the contemplative teenage notebook that
I carry; stones, thigh plaster, all of us smeared with bank shadows & roses
in this quasi-night realm, I slap my glassy skin to see if I am still alive, next to
him, lost long ago, in the mountains, he sings to hummingbirds in the sierra
marsh, something about peace & breath, a delicate antennae   shoots
across the street, across this sacred Huichol straw mat where my mother & I eat
the First corn in the First morning when the First Ones give us knowledge
& love. Puccini blasts out of Molinari's deli, tenors gaze through the reeds,
Tiny Modotti, the acid queen, jaunts into Big Al's, this night, this nest of dried
red corn, the fourth corn—yellow, white mixed, red, the last corn, reddish in
the bulbous air, blistered, Oh, my elder father says, after so many
years dragging his ghost through the valleys, through Sonora &

Chihuahua, through Tijuana & East Los Angeles, from Taos, from
Mesquite through the San Joaquin, kinsman to Zinacantan, to the plague of
ghosts slumped drinking from   illegal grape picking hats & their
long backs spindled in the heat going up like vapor, like their own spliced
trueness, my father sings as he points to me, through the line of Indian
interpreters, President grammarians, Mestizo newsmen, *soldado* shirt
makers, in neon jitters, through this line he comes to me, points beyond the
balcony as he sings

O Tauyaupá
O Tauyaupá
O sacred   sun piece

I come to you now,

                in this form, in this bluish

                        light of elder brother deer,
            Kauyumári,

        I bring these rattles & chicken heads, I bring

        the prayers &   longings of my round village,
        with   their thin fingers they pray to you   too,

through
these passages,

our crystal soul
            shall rise, o Tau o Tau o Tau o Tau, if

we have healed others properly & carefully

            with spirit longing   we shall   rise   to your house,
                he sings

assembled in the dark ancient rings of this sub-realm
in this ring of Nayar

　　　　　　　ravines & alleyways　　　across Río Santiago,

　　　　　　　more villages & towns in their burning shrouds,
　　　　　　　postmodern,　　　　　　levers &

　　　　　　　flesh wheels with
scarves & scars, a flutter of music begins.

Grandfather slaps the deerskin Tepo drum, the amorous leaves

o Tau

o Tau
o Tau yaupá a breeze falls, a gondola of blood, blessed breath

of the wise hummingbird, carry our knowledge
back to us, from afar

　　　　　beyond dead Mexico beyond dead Anahuak, in this perfect
meditation wing, across the greenness,

the *soldado* fury unleashed,　　　　　　　　　　a fuse,
　　　　　　　　　　　　　　　　　　　　　　　a spirit,

in our quixotic leather-patched shoes, this continent   street, club
        of the night, this sub-swiveled bedroom.

        All my tiny awakenings, under Big Al

my bundled mother Lucía innocent
under the serum sack calling out for one more night,

            Tepo drum

                for liberation & destruction, your sacred Tau, our
        shattered eagle & serpent memory, this bracelet of lives tattered
& crossed

        in America, this sub-America, morphined.

Nourish us
                & sweeten us under the fire

                escape. I can see Tepic, I can see San Cristóbal,
                Chenalhó—the ceiba tree swaying over Cozumel

        a sky growing thick roots, under the Los Angeles Freeway, busted
        reddish in the truck tarp

        wedges & venetian blinds open.

notes for "broadway indian"

This canto is dedicated to my Huichol, Cora, Tepehuano, and Mexicanero brothers and sisters of north-central Mexico and particularly to Guadalupe de la Cruz Ríos of El Colorín village in the Nayar Mountains, for her wisdom and hospitality—and in memory of the late Ramón Medina Silva, friend and guide.

::   ::   ::

WIXÁRIKA: Term the Huichols use to refer to themselves, meaning uncertain; may mean "the people."

TATÉI: Mother

TATÉI KUKURUKÚ 'UIMARI: Our Mother Dove Girl, the maize goddess

TEPEHUANO: Neighboring Indian group

KALIWEY: Temple

XIRIKI: Household temple

TAU: Sun

TAUYAUPÁ: Sun Father

KAUYUMÁRI: Deer person, Huichol culture hero

TATEWARÍ: Our Grandfather (Fire)

TAMÁTSI ÉKATEWÁRI: Our Elder Brother Wind

PROMOTOR: Indigenous National Institute (INI) Indian teacher

VERDULERO: Produce truck driver

we are all saying the same thing

angel wrestler (with blond wig)

They come & offer maize,
oat gruel.

Blue-red rooster feathers in a ceramic bowl. Cigarettes, wide mouth.
Incense, bowls. Zircon stones, at times, little see-through rice-paper letters
with diamond shapes, names & sonnets. I hate sonnets. Sestinas are for
pigs. What am I doing up here, next to the Nixon posters? No one listens
to me. My back is about to give, my hands are charred from holding these
yellow candles & chocolate coin nets. The wig is embarrassing. I tell them,
go fishing. Come on, get off your rumps, go fishing, throw a line, tear a loaf
of French into pieces, it's the best bait, you know, dump it into the waves,
hurry, go—*nada*. They kneel for a few seconds, adjust their privates in front
of me, they fondle the chair cushion, the velvet one with 60s embroidery.
Inventory time baby, I yell. Count your cells time! Here's a dream with your
mother's head cut off. What more do you want? It's no use, they don't listen.
The D is missing from your DNA! I sing. Actually my baritone voice is fluid,
prismatic & quite cheeky.

Nada.
They sit there, next to my left wing, scratch the bald spots, trace the welts, dig
reddish splotches behind the feeble ear. My back, I tell you, is about to go.
All I have to honor is my face, the nose is still good, Andalusian, my
wondrous breasts. Listen, I take off my Jim Morrison leather boots &
sprinkle confectionery sugar powder on the soles of my feet. Maybe, I'll leave
a couple of footprints in front of their fishbowl, next to the computer office
door. Just me & the collie, the one they leave behind for the Mercedes. We
fly over the sofa a hundred times, crash against the CD collections stacked like
Byzantine churches. Shhh. Mother goldfish is awake. Her infinite mouth
calls me with fiery halos. The eyes play an aqua minuet with devotion, a tiny
tongue floats out of a cloud, a slow explosion goes into white patches, then
rain, the serenity of black mountains, in strange motion, an infinite tear.

simple poet constructs hunger

Give me Bulgaria,
its demolitions, its contempt for Communism, its pâté of thick-backed
administrators grasping at the old regime.
My nose? You ask. The State has eaten it.

In an apartment
overlooking Dorogomilovsky Market, a homecoming parade
celebrates my return. Three Russian teenagers snap a photo of my face.
A Polaroid in muted tones, a shy type with scarves, then they sit
on a couch at the cafe & stare at a fancy car melting into the afternoon haze.
One of the boys deserted his military unit in Chechnya. They too are hungry;
I can tell by their stiff fingers. The war is over, one says.
Forgiveness or bread?
Punishment or wine? Five thousand march in the iciness, in the ruins.
Searching for my nose with the others, one looks for an ear.

No one notices; Gogol, my dog, leads the way.
Hepatitis & mystery float in the currents of the Aral sea.
Pesticides from the cotton & fishing industries, they say, as the girl
belly bloats with unspoken & hushed desires. Rifle butts
with my ass against a car. Under broken floors.

My clairvoyance fails me.
The spirit drops into a washerwoman's bucket, limp,
weary—the smell of oil & potatoes.

young kuramoto

He was a sad angel, Kuramoto—a family man of eight, on welfare subsidies,
cheese lines & turkey day festivities, on the welfare benefits of his new
nation, a man about town, with a belly & a knack for jokes & tales from
the old country, as a matter of fact he had a way of speaking about the old
country, Suffering—he would call it, out loud, recalling his intimate relations
in that faraway place, he even went as far as meticulously describing his
cubed & boxed luggage, how he hauled it from the shores, all this he would
recount as he entertained his close associates over a small, thick glass of Anise
Del Mono from his village, he played seven-card-no-peek, his favorite,
his face would flush, then in a quick change of mood he would jump
to the iron belly stove & fry quesadillas stuffed with squash flowers—
flores de calabaza—another remnant from the old territories. Kuramoto,
as you can see, was a man with a fond heart full of sunlit pictures, a time
gone.

I've changed my name, he sang one day to his wife, they told me it means
Warrior of the Seven Virtues & as sure as you can toss & swallow the
sweet syrup of anise, he whispers them, one by one, all seven: kindness,
compassion, patience, sacrifice, solitude, contemplation, emptiness, of course,
he could not name them all at once, that in itself was a sin. He could not
admonish his weary-eyed employers, that in itself a trespass, he could not
warn or preach to the local squad of tiny-evil doers, another illusion.
It would cost him in the end; Kuramoto was at a standstill, his game was
an odd net of solitaire—pull against your own hard-won forces, caress
your own trials, smother out the tiny tendrils of your own slippage.
From time to time speak to your children & your lover, mention
the suffering place, this Kuramoto can do, a permissible move.

lord jim

They never found her.
It was her lot. Rómulo said
nobody beats her at Pyramid Palms Realty International.

Nobody messes with her on her own turf.
CarmensouttheresomewhereIdon'tcare. The husband had a bad habit
running his words together when he was at a loss. This wasn't the first time.
Or the second. Out there. She was. True.

In any case, there was a wrought iron gate (this is central to the story).
The fact remains that the dog, that is, the Chihuahua, known for its Aztec
ancestry, its large parietal bone structure & its unassumingly quick attack
due its own predestined fate regarding intimacy & human disintegration,
had a number of telltale signs: red spots, dark
cinnamon reddish, detectives say.

She was on the way, they say. Maybe, Finnochio's—
hangout for all nighthawks in Tillamook County;
you could find her clientele there usually sipping a gin gimlet.
Finnocchio's? Not a chance.

I've got the report.
Last seen at Lord Jim's—
the quintessential late night spot for tawdry pre-divorce annunciations.
Being a real estate broker, a poet of sorts (she always
carried a book by Anaïs Nin, with journals & neon-colored
crayons, of course), she was a master—
engaging the opponent in arguments about faith, trust & whether
or not she should renounce all her belongings, the job-job
& immediately enlist at the local Zen center.

Highly unlikely,
Rómulo, her sporty husband's lawyer, told me.
In another realm: grass covers her eyes.
She picks away at the earth.

Out. Going out she was.
Someone found a pair of bifocals left at the restaurant.
      Witness # 1 says:
      "Carrera, two-tone wash, gray, with green stripe frames."
Notunlikecarmentoleaveme. Rómulo.
He knew the husband. Carmen. She knew. Both did.

five directions to my house

1. Go back to the grain yellow hills where the broken speak of elegance
2. Walk up to the canvas door, the short bed stretched against the clouds
3. Beneath the earth, an ant writes with the grace of a governor
4. Blow, blow Red Tail Hawk, your hidden sleeve—your desert secrets
5. You are there, almost, without a name, without a body, go now
6. I said five, said five like a guitar says six.

i found myself in the studio of a tabla master

for Genny Lim

In Varanasi, the spirit waters of the Ganges burn death at my feet
bones, rags, ancient pyres, the first fleck of namelessness, the bodies
go up in singular smoke, in greenish ribbons, a woman at my right,
her left leg bent in the pose of fulfillment, as if about to dance or step
into birth, or dawn, a faded tiger skin at her hips, the Ganges takes her,
healers let go of the child body, with the eyes complete in mute light
the villagers wash, again, lift water to their faces, five counts, five chants
may Vajrapani return as the last sage, may we learn from the Ruru deer,
her melodious voice for the hunter, the one who arrows only himself,
sing out to Mila, who drank nettle soup for years, until his arms, gaunt
face were as the plant in his meals, the flavor of stillness, a sitar
divides the smoke & jeers, a skull bowl, a curved knife in the wave
dance among the lotuses, a reddish conch shell opens, it is an ear
my breast, my hand, a forgotten & abandoned scarf that bellows
the tabla is before me, in my honor they are saying, the players drum
mountain shapes, the child goes down below the horizon, the tiny hiss
flute & serpent leads, charred leaves, my lives into lines on the waters.

we are all saying the same thing

—after Szymborska

Yeti come down. The escape is over—the earthquake
mixes the leaves into an exotic pattern.

You slide down the precipice & spit.
You chew on a Tibetan prayer wheel.

This is our city with the bridge in flames, call it Desire.
This is our mountain, hear its umber harness shiver, call it Time.

& this old woman beating a bluish rag
with her shredded hands—call her now,

call her with your honey-like voices.
She is the sky you were after, that immeasurable breath
in every one of us.

We are all saying the same thing, Yeti.
We lift our breast & speak of fire, then ice.

We press into our little knotted wombs
wonder about our ends, then, our beginnings.

about the author

Juan Felipe Herrera is a graduate of sixties street poetics, campesino migrant treks, and multimedia political theater experiments. He has founded percussion and jazz poetry ensembles, Chicano teatros, and poetry brigades, and has taken his various word troupes across the United States and into Mexico and Latin America for the last thirty years. He has served as editor of a number of groundbreaking small-press magazines such as *Red Trapeze*, *El Tecolote Literario*, *Gato's Journal*, *Bovine Interventions*, *Citybender*, and university reviews, including *Vortice* and *Metamorfosis*. He holds degrees from the University of California-Los Angeles, Stanford University, and the University of Iowa, and has received numerous awards for his writing. He lives in Fresno, California, with his wife, the performance artist Margarita Luna Robles, and children.